The Gospel
of the Bleeding Woman

Poems

The Gospel
of the Bleeding Woman

Poems

Katie Manning

POINT LOMA
PRESS

WIPF & STOCK · Eugene, Oregon

The Gospel of the Bleeding Woman

Point Loma Press Series

Point Loma Press
3900 Lomaland Dr.
San Diego, CA 92106

Wipf and Stock Publishers
199 W. 8th Ave., Suite 3
Eugene, OR 97401

www.pointloma.edu/pointlomapress

www.wipfandstock.com

ISBN 13: 978-1-62564-097-0

Table of Contents

Foreword for Point Loma Press Series

Point Loma Press was founded in 1992 to provide a publishing outlet for faculty and to serve the distinct theological mission of Point Loma Nazarene University (San Diego, CA). Over time the press has grown to publish authors from a wider range of institutional backgrounds, but its core mission remains the same: to encourage and extend a distinctly Wesleyan theological perspective on various topics and issues for the church today. Most Point Loma Press books are theological in scope, though many are quite practical in their focus, and some address non-theological topics but from a Wesleyan theological perspective. All Point Loma Press books are written with a broad audience in mind, intended to contribute effectively to contemporary scholarship while also being accessible to pastors, laypersons, and students alike. Our hope is that our new collaboration with Wipf & Stock Publishers will continue to allow us to expand our audience for the important topics and perspective of our work.

Point Loma Press welcomes any submissions that meet these criteria. Inquiries should be directed to PointLomaPress@pointloma.edu or 619-849-2359. When submitting, please provide rationale for how your work supports the mission of the Point Loma Nazarene University Wesleyan Center to articulate distinctly Wesleyan themes and trajectories.

Acknowledgments

Special thanks to the journal editors who first published the following poems, sometimes in earlier forms.

Fickle Muses: "The Flesh Made Word" and "Where Death Is Not an Is"
So to Speak: "The Gospel of the Bleeding Woman" and
                "The Resurrection of Nura"
Trivia: "First Blood," "Well," and "The History of Bleeding"

Thanks also to Hadara Bar-Nadav, Michelle Boisseau, Ki Russell, Rashad Givhan, Katie Galvin, and Piper Abernathy for their invaluable feedback on these poems; to Mark Mann for his thoughtful editorial suggestions and great enthusiasm for this collection; and to Jon Manning for his translations, multiple readings, and constant encouragement.

I.

First Blood

       Just dawn. The warmth
wakes me. I feel wet
and ashamed
       but then I know.
I bolt up, look
down at the cloth.
       A dark tide pool
       spreads out
from the center—
a red sun rises
       where life begins.

Seven Weeks Later

The tears won't flow
from my face the way blood
flows from my womb.
The current continues

daily down my legs
though I have begged
the God whose temple
I may not enter to sew

me closed. Once,
they say, he turned
an Egyptian sea to blood
and back to water.

I don't believe this now.
The blood remains
and never turns. My tide
moves ever out and out.

The Doctors Advise

She has—
      She is—
            She miscarried—
a leaking heart.
      an abnormality.
            a demon.

She must have—
      She could have—
            She has sinned.
      touched herself.
eaten unclean meat.

Bleed her arms each day.
      Kill one goat a week.
            At the next full moon, float face
            down in the center of the sea.

Passover

They tell me my body
is impure.
I am not the same girl
who scoured the house for leaven
on her hands and knees.

I am not the same girl
who ate the *Pesach*[1] meat
before morning, careful
not to break
tradition with her teeth.

If I lived in Egypt when death
floated past, I wouldn't slaughter
the lamb, smear blood
over the door. One bleeding
body per house
must be enough for God.

---

[1] Passover; also refers to the sacrificial lamb

Well

Only at night now do I drop
my bucket down in the darkness,

watch as the moon rises
silver in the water, swaying

on the surface like a fallen
feather and growing larger

with each tug on the rope.
I raise my eyes and lift

the liquid to the sky.
A shiver thrills my body

though the night is warm,
and I drink. The coolness

tingles my lips. I pour
the rest over my head

and let it rush
down my breasts.

Blood, dirt, and water stream
down my legs, pool

at my feet. I am clean,
almost. I lower my bucket

again and pull the rope
more gently, slowly

savoring the sight
of each glowing ripple.

I grow tired, dripping
red and silver as I go.

The Story of Warmth and Light

My only sister is Chuma—
warmth. She was born
on a summer afternoon
and never stopped smiling
as a child, even in sleep.
She became a woman
a year before her older sister
and married Simon,
who smelled of fish
and laughed loudly.
She holds a son in each arm
and still smiles
though her husband left
his boat to follow a teacher.
She hugs me in secret.

And I am Nura—*light.*
The morning sun fell
across my face when I tore
from mother's womb.
My sister and light
are what touch me now.

Stone

I sit beside our *miqweh*[2]
and long to dive in, head
first, and hold my breath
until I burst for air or
let myself drown.

But I am unclean,
so filthy that pure
water can't fix
me now. I fill
my stone bowl

from the bath—
father says
I can't infect
stone—and I
wipe my body

down, rub
hard until
my thighs
are red
without
blood.

I scrub.
I scrub
but will
not dis-
appear.

---

2   A bath or small pool. Many Jewish families in Galilee at the time of Jesus had
these in their homes for purification purposes.

An Issue

I bleed on a mound of cloth beside
a window. I bleed and weave
fishing nets of living fabric. I watch
the sun rise and set, children play

and fight. I've learned the rhythms
of day and night these 12 years. Once
I had a name. But I bleed,
and the blood blots everything.

The children in the street call
Bleeding woman! and laugh.
I pray that God, if He is a God
of mercy, will strike the mockers

dumb—that when they run
to tell their parents in gestures
they've lost their tongues, their
mouths will issue only blood.

First Sight

I am weaving at the window

    when a crowd comes

        down the street—a group

        of men. My sister's husband

in front walks beside

a man in a simple white cloak—

this must be that rabbi.

        The crowd pulses

           forward. They seem

           to be one body. Then

I hear voices. Someone says,

    "She's in here."

I sit unmoving in my chair,

not daring even to breathe.

           A distant door opens.

Another moment

    and the house fills

with gasps and cheers.

The teacher has healed my

mother's fever. She shouts thanks

to him above

the din. Dishes clink

loudly in the kitchen

as if they too would shout,

and mother cooks

for the crowd. The scent

of the best lamb creeps

into my room, but nothing

else comes or goes. I close

my eyes and see myself

out there, part of the group—

feel that man in the white cloak

touch my skin, heal

my broken body too.

The History of Bleeding

The first year taught herself to swim
while she drowned
the second denied everything   the third
locked herself in a room and refused
to move
the fourth slept all the time
the fifth
dreamed of a baby wrapped
in white cloth
covered in blood
the sixth traced her name in dirt
a hundred times   the seventh
baked bread daily
the eighth weaved fishing nets
and despised the smell of fish
the ninth and tenth dug a mass grave
for hope   the eleventh
filled it with blood
and the twelfth
stole a piece of God

The Gospel of the Bleeding Woman

"Just then a woman who had been subject to bleeding for twelve years came up behind him..." –Matthew 9:20

"And a woman was there who had been subject to bleeding for twelve years." –Mark 5:25 and Luke 8:43

I touched his cloak. This much is certain. Suddenly I had no name. Suddenly I inhabited a body split in three. I had been blood's subject for 12 years. I had seen doctors. One time doctors didn't exist. One time my voice didn't exist. Other times I heard voices in my head. Then I touched his white cloak. I explained myself. He knew without asking. Always he called me *Daughter, Daughter, Daughter*, and said *Your faith has healed you.* Then he said *Go in peace.* Then he said *Go in peace and be freed from your suffering.* Then he said nothing and walked off to find a dead girl. I touched his cloak. Suddenly I was alone. Suddenly I didn't exist. I walked home in a trance and fell asleep with my sandals on. I didn't wake up in time to see how our stories would end.

II.

Transport

In the back of a strange
silver tube   speeding
through a dark tunnel as if
free and trapped at once   I turn
to the back window   see a wave
of blood rise   gaining height
and speed   the wave curls
    blood and metal mingle
I shriek with the brakes
    close my eyes

        red   glowing red

I force my lids open and see
sunlight shine more brightly
than ever before   not a trace
of blood anywhere
even the tunnel   gone

The Resurrection of Nura

Just dawn. The noise
wakes me.
I wonder why
I'm wearing sandals
and how I know the word *clock*.
I bolt up, look
out the window: yellow cars
scream on the street below,
yellow leaves fill the park.
Then I remember he told me
Your faith has healed you.
My temples throb, and I think—
What faith?

Nura Remembers Peter

Some will remember
the lake-top stroll,
how he sank under ungodly
waves   some will
recall the words *I do not know him*
and the cock's crow piercing
the darkened dawn

but now   when I walk
through midtown at top speed
avoiding elbows
and blown-out umbrellas,
I recall the brother-in-law who pushed
me through the crowd against the law
to take my last chance   and touch God

God's Sense of Humor

Here I am, confused
because I know
too much. I've been
healed, transported
to a new life, literally.

I went from Galilee
to New York faster
than an airplane
could've done (and
I know what airplanes
are, inexplicably).

I have a life centuries
after I was born:
an apartment, a job
as a librarian (specializing
in history and religion),
a dog, cable television...

Somehow I know exactly
what God has done to me,
but—some things never
change—have no idea why.
Life opens before and behind
me, and every page is blank.

Nura Goes to the Store

I like to shop at Wal-Mart
where every aisle says *always*.
I walk along humming
The Girl from Ipanema—
I sing *The Girl from Galilee*
in my head—and ponder
the signs: *Always Low Prices,*
Always. But this sign
is just a few months old. This
store, only a few years.
Most of all—I've reached
the aisle of feminine products—
these maxi-pads in the bright
blue plastic case weren't
always around for my use,
and I needed them
in many ways at least.

Nura Finds Herself

Sometimes I spend the afternoon
searching for myself
online: "bleeding woman bible"

      ▪ <u>MIRACLES ATTRIBUTED TO JESUS</u>
I had long-term bleeding.
It could've been *menorrhagia*
(hyperlink to definition:
a heavy and painful period),
but many scholars
think the 12-year duration
means hemophilia—my blood
just couldn't contain itself.

      ▪ <u>LIST OF NAMES FOR THE BIBLICAL NAMELESS</u>
Some of us answered to "Hey, you!"
and had no existence outside stories.
I collected Jesus' blood on a cloth
at his crucifixion. My name might
have been Berenice or Veronica.

Let's forget my bleeding, forget
that Matthew, Mark, and Luke
forgot my name. I search
once more for "Nura."

      ▪ <u>NURA LULUYEVA</u>
The Chechan nurse sold
roadside strawberries to Russian
soldiers. They paid with a sack
over her head and a mallet to her skull.

■   NURA NAL
Dream Girl, comic book character
and thirtieth-century super-hero.
She dies in battle despite
her narcoleptic power to see
the future. In newer versions, she
always reappears, alive and dreaming.

In the MoMA

after Nancy Spero's "Notes in Time"

Women dominate

    the walls:

    collages with cream

backdrops and curvaceous

silhouettes,

    black and yellow

faded newsprint.

    I squint

at the nearest words:

    the perfect woman tears
    to pieces when she loves...

I imagine Nietzsche

snarling, mouth

    hidden by mustache,

    though I can't decide

    if he means she rips

herself or her lover.

No blood spots

here, no tidal moons.

No need when words leak

red at their edges and tear

flesh at first sight.

I back to the bench

and watch perfect pieces

mate in museum light.

Telling It Like It Is

I pick a book
off the shelf: *Telling
It Like It Is: The Truth
About All the Women
of the Bible.* Apparently
I was a widow
with cancer. Where do
they get this stuff?
Apparently I had great
faith, yet was frightened
when Jesus noticed me.
And most of all,
the author notes, The
Woman with the Blood
"didn't even thank Him."

I touched. He asked.
The crowd pushed on.
When I raised my eyes
to his, I stared into
the dark knot of a tree
and found life staring back.

The Flesh Made Word
(Nura's Translation)

They found God praying to himself in a garden. One man
kissed him on the cheek. Amen. It was finished. They
marched him off to watch the judge wash his hands.
They thorned his crown and flayed his back, walked him
up a slope of skulls and nailed him to a T. Some men
bled his side and gambled for his clothes. Some women
cried for themselves. The God held his breath. It was
finished. Amen. Nothing left but to gather his body
between sheets and lay him in a book to rise again.

After the Rain in Central Park

Blown-out umbrellas pile
in bins like birds with broken
necks, a terrier trots over to piss
on the trash, the wind chafes
my cheeks and shoves
my breath back. A pale woman
lopes by, holding a coffee cup
and a lit cigarette, a cell phone
between shoulder and ear—

A familiar man steps off
the path carrying a black case.
He settles on a bench and reveals
a silver trumpet. I hear the Lord
play: *Love is now the stardust
of yesterday, the music
of the years gone by.* Bare
branches stir. A leaf
of paper twirls in time.

Where Death Is Not an Is

after Brian Henry

I met Jesus the next day
at the Life Café. "Call me
J now," he said. "People
lock me up when I say

I am God." He pulled
back his sleeves to show
the marks on his arms
from recent shots. I asked

what I could do. "Just lie
low," he said between
bites of falafel. "Dead
is the way the world wants

us. People hate to feel
alive." We ate in silence
for a while. Then I asked,
"What happens to us?"

He wiped his young hands
and stood to leave. "We are
finished," and kissed my cheek.
I put my hand on his arm

and told him the scars would be
beautiful when they healed.

Notes

"Seven Weeks Later" – The story of the first plague on Egypt is from Exodus 7.

"The Doctors Advise" – Mark 5:26: "She had suffered a great deal under the care of many doctors and had spent all she had, yet instead of getting better she grew worse."

"Passover" owes its ritual details to Tracey Rich's highly informative website *Judaism 101* at www.jewfaq.org.

"The Story of Warmth and Light" – I chose the names Chuma and Nura from the list of Aramaic names on thinkbabynames.com. The bleeding woman is unnamed in the Bible and nothing is known about her family. I developed the fictional theory that she was Simon Peter's sister-in-law.

"Stone" – Jonathan L. Reed's *Archaeology and the Galilean Jesus: A Re-examination of the Evidence* contains information on stone vessels, *miqwaoth*, and ritual purity.

"An Issue" – In the King James Version of the Bible, the woman is described as having "an issue of blood twelve years."

"First Sight" – Jesus heals Peter's mother-in-law in Matthew 8, Mark 1, and Luke 4.

"The Gospel of the Bleeding Woman" layers details from all three of the gospel accounts that include the unnamed woman's story. The epigraph verses come from Today's New International Version.

"Nura Remembers Peter" – The story of Jesus and Peter walking on water comes from Matthew 14. The story of Peter denying Jesus appears in Matthew 26, Mark 14, Luke 22, and John 18. The story of Peter getting the bleeding woman through the crowd is my own creation.

"Nura Finds Herself" includes search results from www.wikipedia.org.

"Telling It Like It Is" – Mary E. Townsend's *Telling It Like It Is: The Truth About All the Women of the Bible* especially notes that the bleeding woman didn't thank Jesus, and Townsend uses this example as a caution to her readers to always thank God.

"The Flesh Made Word (Nura's Translation)" is a collision of all four biblical passion narratives with some altered details and added flare.

"After the Rain in Central Park" contains lyrics by Mitchell Parish from the jazz standard "Stardust."

"Where Death Is Not an Is" echoes lines from Brian Henry's *Quarantine* in its title and text.

About the Author

K atie Manning, upon first seeing a rhinoceros at the zoo at age 2, declared to her mother, "I want to be one of those when I grow up!" Although she has yet to realize this dream, she is happy to live with her husband and son in Southern California, where she is employed as an Assistant Professor of English at Azusa Pacific University. Her poetry has been published in *New Letters*, *PANK*, *The Pedestal Magazine,* and *Poet Lore*, among other journals and anthologies. Find her online at www. katiemanningpoet.com.